Ic '

Contents	Page

written by John Lockyer

Icebergs are big lumps of ice.
They float in very cold seas.

iceberg

Some icebergs are as big as our houses. Others are as big as tall buildings!

glacier

All icebergs are made
of fresh water.
Icebergs can come from
ice rivers on the land.
The ice rivers are
called glaciers.

4

Icebergs are made when big
lumps of an ice river fall
into the sea.

Some icebergs look round.
Icebergs can be other shapes.
Some icebergs look like very
big blocks.

Some icebergs look like mountains. Other icebergs have big, long tunnels.

Only the top of an iceberg shows. Most of an iceberg is under the water.

Ships that go in cold seas
have to keep away from
big icebergs.

The ice in an iceberg has lots of small bubbles of air. The air bubbles make the iceberg float.

floating

The wind and the tide make icebergs move.

Icebergs keep getting smaller as they float in the sea.

melting

The sun, the wind, and the sea water make the icebergs melt away.

Seals and penguins live on big icebergs.
They dive into the sea to find their food.
Icebergs are floating homes.